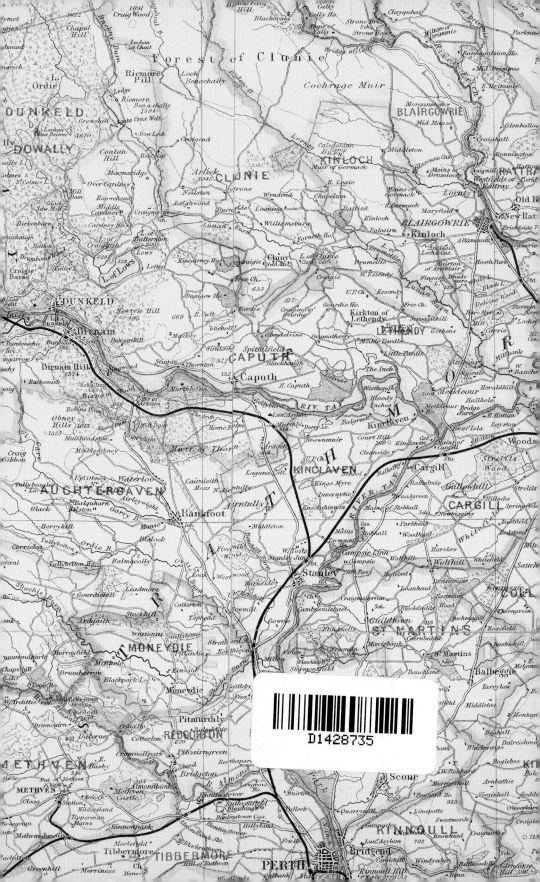

Reflections Loch Pulney, Dunkeld.

Loch Pulney, Dunkeld

Along the A9
The Great North Road

Ailean MacDonald

Perth & Kinross Libraries

ISBN 0 905452 32 1

Published by
Perth & Kinross Libraries
AK Bell Library
York Place
Perth
PH2 8EP

PERTH &
KINROSS
COUNCIL

Printed by
Cordfall Ltd
0141 572 0878

FALLS OF TUMMEL, PITLOCHRY.

92049.

A salmon leaping the Falls of Tummel, Pitlochry

The A9 is Scotland's Great North Road, running from the heart of the country, dividing the old county of Perthshire, following General Wade's original road north to Inverness and taking travellers to the edge of the country at John o' Groats itself.

The main stretch passed through Perthshire and not so very long ago a driver leaving Perth who was unfortunate enough to be stuck behind a lorry could well find himself facing the same number plate on the Drumochter Pass. The road passed through some of Scotland's grandest scenery, small towns and picturesque villages, and though it has been refurbished, improved and restructured to pass centres of habitation, there are still stretches where one can understand the claims that the A9 is not only the longest, but the loveliest road in Scotland.

From Victorian times and the coming of the railways, every village shop and post office sold postcards as a natural part of the tourist trade and a souvenir of their pride in their own identity. This trade was given a new lease of life in the 1930s when motoring became a holiday and weekend pursuit. And the trend continued well into the 1960s, as motoring became more popular.

Perth and Kinross Libraries has an unrivalled collection of these postcards, gathered from all over the country and covering every corner of Perthshire. Though the messages on the back are often interesting and amusing, especially those sent before telephones were common, it is the pictures that concern us here. This is a small selection.

Every library holds collections, but Perth's is unique because of its range and breadth. It is a collection that has been assembled rather than deliberately gathered, covering Old Perthshire from the Trossachs and the site of the battle of Sheriffmuir in the south to the Drumochter Pass, from the Strathearn lowlands to the hills of Glen Shee and the Devil's Elbow. And, of course, there's Perth itself. Some of Scotland's grandest names and loveliest scenery are in this collection, memorably pictured by anonymous photographers and often chosen by strangers who happen to be passing.

This book is the first sampling. Other parts of the collection will follow.

Ailean MacDonald

Bridge of Garry

In summer fields were said to be white with cloth when William Sandeman set up a dyeing business in LUNCARTY. His business merged with the Pullar family to establish Pullars of Perth, the original dry cleaning business and one of the town's main employees. Professor Archibald Sandeman, founder of Perth's Sandeman Library, was William Sandeman's son.

The Dam Dyke, Luncarty

For many from Glasgow, Edinburgh and beyond, **LUNCARTY** was little more than a pleasant holiday village. Yet this is where Scotland acquired an emblem. In 990 the sleeping Scots would have been surprised by an army of invading Danes but for the fact that a barefoot Danish soldier stood on a thistle in the dark.

Main Street, Bankfoot.

The quiet village of **BANKFOOT** is clearly visible from the **A9**, at the foot of a brae leaving Perth where traffic can often slow to a crawl.

Two miles north of **BANKFOOT** is the start of the Highland Boundary fault, where the landscape changes from rolling farms to wooded mountains.

Backmill Road, Bankfoot

B.107

Stanley Church from Percy Street, Stanley.

B.36.

STANLEY is one of Perthshire's planned villages, conceived in the early 1780s to house the workforce for Stanley Mill. The village was built by the Earls of Derby, who were related by marriage to the Dukes of Atholl, and given the Derby family name.

Stanley Mills and River Tay.

B.2

The original **MURTHLY CASTLE** dates from the fourteenth century, but in the early 1830s Sir William Drummond Stewart began work on a new castle which, he claimed, would rival the Duke of Atholl's seat at Blair Atholl. The new Murthly Castle was never completed and the shell was demolished in 1949.

STANLEY cotton mills were established by a consortium which included the fourth Duke of Atholl, local businessmen and Richard Arkwright, inventor of the spinning jenny, which had revolutionised cotton production. Arkwright soon left, but Stanley Mill was the area's main employer for more than 200 years. The mill closed in 1989, following a major fire, but Historic Scotland stepped in to save an important part of Scotland's industrial architectural heritage.

Murthly Hospital, Murthly, Perthshire.

The former county mental hospital still dominates the landscape. Built in 1864, it has been greatly enlarged, though judicious tree planting kept the buildings and its inmates well secluded.

The River Isla joins the Tay at **KINCLAVEN**, which takes its name from *caen*, a headland; *kil*, a church; and *abhiam*, a river; indicating that there has been a place of worship here for centuries. This is Kinclaven Church, the oldest United Presbyterian Church in Scotland. Kinclaven Parish Church was built in 1848.

Kinclaven Church.

KINCLAVEN FERRY ON THE TAY.

KINCLAVEN Ferry has been a vital crossing point certainly since mediaeval times and probably before, given the Roman camp at nearby Inchtuthill, as well as the many surrounding signal forts and stations. Now there are two bridges, one across the Tay, the other across the Isla.

KINCLAVEN BRIDGE FROM W

4431 CAPUTH FROM THE HILL.

The tiny village of **CAPUTH** is centre of a parish which stretches from the north bank of the Tay to Butterstone Loch and Loch of the Lowes.

The Lunan Burn rises in the Grampians and runs for fourteen miles into the River Isla, passing through the Loch of Craiglush, Loch of the Lowes, Butterstone Loch, Loch of Clunie, Marlee Loch, Rae Loch and Fingask Loch.

Loch of the Lowes is now an osprey breeding ground, part of a nature reserve owned by the Scottish Wildlife Trust with excellent facilities to view the nesting birds.

Birnam and the Lochs

In Birnam Glen

Until the 1860s and the coming of the railway, BIRNAM was a wood, a hill, an estate and an idea which became a village which should, we are repeatedly reminded, be properly called Little Dunkeld.

The village is famous throughout the world because Shakespeare has Birnam Wood marching to Dunsinane. Locals call the place *Dun-sin-ann*, which ruins the bard's meter.

In Birnam Glen.

Part of "Great Birnam Wood"

THE MILLS, TROCHRY. 808

TROCHRY. 806

The Hermitage, Dunkeld.

8019. J.V.

Half a mile off the A9 and along a woodland trail is the HERMITAGE, also known as Ossian's Hall, a classical stone summer house built in 1758 by the third Duke of Atholl. Burns came here in 1787, a trip which included a visit to Niel Gow at INVER, and William and Dorothy Wordsworth came in 1803. The Hermitage walls originally had mirrors which were positioned to magnify the spectacle of the tumbling River Braan in full spate, just as the domed ceiling is designed to amplify the noise.

The River Braan runs from Loch Freuchie in Glen Quaich, above the Sma' Glen and Amulree, and runs for twelve miles to join the Tay at INVER, passing Rumbling Bridge, the Hermitage and the village of Trochry, whose farmhouse was famous for doubling as a post office.

Neil Gow's Cottage, Inver

Niel Gow was born near **INVER** in 1727. Through the brilliance of his playing and his compositions he became the best known of all Scottish fiddlers whose method and style became established as the correct way to play, thanks in no small part to his son Nathaniel, a composer who published several volumes of his own and his father's music.

INVER is also the birthplace and home of Charles Macintosh, who was also a composer and fiddle player, as well as a naturalist, whose expertise was admired by Beatrix Potter, who met Charlie during many summer holidays spent with her family at Dalguise. She reputedly used him as the model for Mr MacGregor.

ATHOLL MEMORIAL FOUNTAIN, DUNKELD

DUNKELD is clustered round the Cathedral and has gone through at least two regenerations. The first was after the Battle of Killiecrankie, when the victorious Jacobites beseiged the Cathedral and burned the town. The rebuilt Dunkeld was later restored by the National Trust for Scotland.

021

. AT DUNKELD—JUDGES LTD

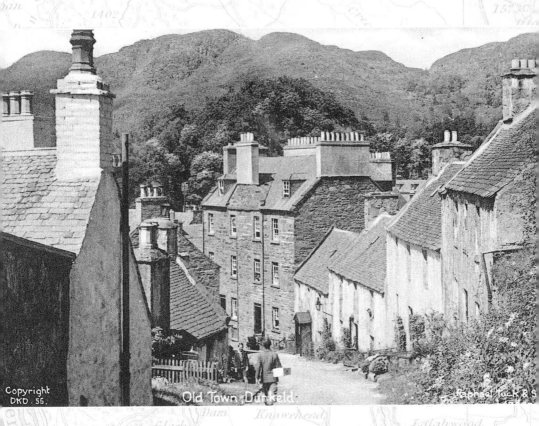

Old Town, Dunkeld.

Before General Wade began his road building programme there was no road north of DUNKELD. This was a frontier town. It took the Duke of Atholl's servants thirteen hours to carry him from Dunkeld to Blair Castle by sedan chair, a distance of seventeen miles.

It seems certain that the Pictish King Conal built a monastery at DUNKELD for St Columba, who spent six months preaching in the area and is commemorated locally at St Colume's Well. Dunkeld became a place of pilgrimage when Kenneth MacAlpin moved some of Columba's bones from Iona.

The present building began in the middle of the twelfth century when King David I elevated Dunkeld to a cathedral. The choir was the east end of the building was first to be completed, followed by the south porch, the chapter house and finally, in 1506, the 46 foot clocktower.

The building took more than 250 years to complete and was in use for less than 60, for in 1560, at the height of the Reformation, the altars and idolatrous images ordered to be removed from the Cathedral and burned. The Privy Council also ordered there should be no unnecessary damage to the

Dunkeld Cathedral from River

9674. THE NAVE, DUNKELD - JUDGES LTD

doors, windows, furniture, glass and metalwork. The mob ignored their instructions and tore the place apart.

In 1600 the Choir was re-roofed, the first of several repairs. The rest of the building remains a roofless shell.

ROHALLION estate is on the east side of Birnam Hill. Buffalo Hill, which rises above Rohallion Loch, gets its name from the buffalo which were imported by Sir William Drummond of Murthly. Having spent some time in Canada, he brought buffaloes back to Scotland, with Indians to look after them. The Indians died of pneumonia, but the buffalo prospered, the last being shot at the end of the nineteenth century.

Rohallion is the name of a poem by Violet Jacob:

> *There isna a hoose that could haud me*
>> *Frae here tae the sea*
> *When the wind frae the braes o' Rohallion*
>> *Comes creepin' tae me;*
> *And never a lowe frae the ingle*
>> *Can draw like the trail an' the shine*
> *O' the stars i' the loch o' Rohallion*
>> *A fitstep o' mine.*

Violet Jacob's poem has been given a new lease of life as a song with a tune by Jim Reid, who has done a similar conversion for works by the other Angus poets, Helen B. Cruickshank and Marion Angus.

Nigel Tranter advises, 'It is a good idea, if the traveller has a little time to spare when heading north or south in the mid-Tay Valley, to take the road B898, along the west side of the river instead of the A9.'*

This road passes through DALGUISE, an area once famous for its orchards. Mr and Mrs Rupert Potter and their children Bertram and Beatrix were regular visitors to the area, returning years after year, though not always to the same accommodation. Some of Beatrix's characters can be traced to the area. Mrs Tiggywinkle was almost certainly based on Kitty MacDonald, a Dalguise washerwoman.

The Queen's Scotland: The Heartland.

GREETINGS from

Charleston.

A Picturesque Corner of Belfield.

Dalguise House, the S.A.B.C. Training Conference & Camping Centre.

DALGUISE

The Road to Aberfeldy.

Because it was founded by St Columba, people believed Dunkeld would be immune from the Great Plague of 1500. So that the town would not be over-run, Bishop George Brown settled the refugees in DOWALLY, and so that they would not lack religious attention he elevated the village to a parish with its own church, dedicated to St Anne.

Dowally Village.

The original inn at GUAY was built by the Bishop of Dunkeld in 1340 as a resting place for travellers and visitors. It was abandoned at the Reformation.

Jacobite refugees were said to have lived in the caves on the hills along the Haugh of Kilmorlich, which runs from Kindallachan to Ballinluig. More recently, Kindallachan had its own sheep market.

BIT OF KINDALLACHAN Nº 605

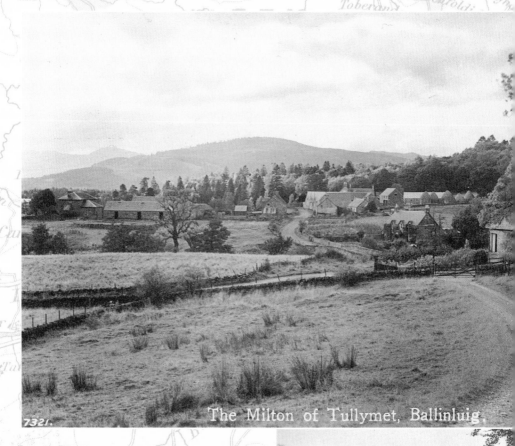

The Milton of Tullymet, Ballinluig.

TULLIMET is the birthplace of Red Rob Mackintosh, another renowned Perthshire fiddler and composer, whose works are in the Atholl Collection, housed at the AK Bell Library in Perth.

THE VILLAGE, BALLINLUIG.

BALLINLUIG was the railway junction for a line which branched off to Aberfeldy. There are two Ballinluigs, less than five miles apart. One, the former junction, is on the A9. The other, pictured here, is five miles east of Aberfeldy.

Though the village of **MOULIN** has largely been absorbed by Pitlochry, it is a far older place. Straddling the road to Kirkmichael and Glenshee, the village has a hotel with its own brewery and a church which Columba (521-97) is said to have founded in 590, making it the oldest in Atholl. Stones in the kirkyard are more recent. One slab shows a mediaeval, long-handled sword, another has the Maltese Cross of a Crusading knight.

BEN VRACKIE means 'speckled hill' because of the white quartz rocks which used to be scattered across its slopes and which were visible from a distance. Almost all the rocks were removed towards the end of the nineteenth century to enhance Pitlochry houses and gardens.

MOULIN AND BEN-Y-VRACKIE.   B.7

Ben Vrackie from the Moulin Road. Pitlochry

38

Pitlochry from Craigour

CRAIGOWER, or 'the goat's rock' lies due north of Pitlochry. Now owned by the National Trust for Scotland, it was a beacon hill, used, it is thought, to signal messages between Dunkeld and Blair Atholl.

PITLOCHRY AND BEN-Y-VRACKIE

MAIN STREET, PITLOCHRY.

PITLOCHRY is one of Scotland's main holiday resorts and touring centres. And though the A9 now passes the edge of the town, the road used to run through Pitlochry, making it a notorious bottleneck.

MAIN STREET, PITLOCHRY.

The Black Spout waterfall is a product of the Eradour Burn, which tumbles through Black Spout Wood and feeds the Eradour Distillery, the smallest in Scotland, at the foot of the brae.

THE CUILC AND BEN-Y-VRACKIE, PITLOCHRY

OCHRY FESTIVAL THEATRE, SCOTLAND'S THEATRE IN THE HILLS.   B.422

PITLOCHRY FESTIVAL THEATRE runs from May to October with a repertory of six or seven plays. Founded in 1951, Scotland's Theatre in the Hills played in a tent within a tent, the inner tent being the auditorium with the foyer and restaurant in the space between the canvases. A semi-permanent home was found in what was the town's ice rink and the present custom-built theatre was opened in 1979.

The only pond in Pitlochry, apart from the remnants of mill ponds, is the CUILC, whose name derives from the Gaelic for sedge.

.7668. THE NEW SUSPENSION BRIDGE OVER LOCH FASKALLY, PITLOCHRY.

The Hydro-Electric Scheme was undertaken in the aftermath of the Second World War with the intention of bringing electricity to every home in the Highlands. It altered the landscape forever.

In March, 1945, a Pitlochry Protest Committee was formed. They objected to Loch Tummell being raised, the Falls of Tummell being reduced, the loss of Clunie Bridge and the fact that the town's recreation ground would be sunk beneath the newly created Loch Faskally.

Five years later the **PITLOCHRY DAM** and **FISH LADDER** was opened and the power switched on.

PITLOCHRY HYDRO DAM

4397. PITLOCHRY DAM - JUDGES LTD.

Hydro electric dam on Loch Faskally

LOCH FASKALLY, PITLOCHRY.

46

THE GREAT NORTH ROAD AT TIGH-NA-GEAT, PITLOCHRY (THE CENTRE OF SCOTLAND)

In 1564, Mary Queen of Scots passed through Moulin on her way to Blair Castle. She is said to have visited the ferryman's house at the southern end of the Pass of Killiecrankie, then known as *BALNAFUIRT*, the house of the ford, and found that the strings of her harp were broken. The ferryman, who happened to be a harp player, repaired the instrument and from then the house has been known as *tigh-na-geat*, the house of the harp string.

   Tigh-na-Geat is one of many places which claims to be the centre of Scotland.

THE PASS OF KILLIECRANKIE FROM THE GREAT NORTH ROAD.

48

KILLIECRANKIE is one of the famous names of Scotland, renowned for its history and scenery. The A9 now rises above the River Garry, by-passing the village and the deeply wooded gorge.

THE GREAT NORTH ROAD AT KILLIECRANKIE.

207965 JV

The **BATTLE** of **KILLIECRANKIE** was fought on 27 July 1689, between the forces of William of Orange, who had been newly brought to the throne, and the exiled Jacobite King James VII and II. The government forces were led by General Mackay and the Jacobites by Graham of Claverhouse.

Bonnie Dundee won the battle, but fell at the moment of victory. Two thousand government troops were killed or captured for a loss of 900 Highlanders, though with Dundee's death the victory was fruitless and that Jacobite campaign soon ended.

SOLDIER'S LEAP, PASS OF KILLIECRANKIE.

The Soldier's Leap (indicated by curve) can still be seen down by the river. Donald McBean, a redcoat, jumped 18 feet across the river to escape the pursuing Jacobites. Others, it is said, were not so agile, or lucky.

Pass of Killiecrankie

MARIE CORELLI (1855-1924) was the pseudonym of Mary Mackay, whose father Charles Mackay was a well known collector and arranger of Scots songs. She originally studied music, but at the age of 30 turned to fiction, producing a highly successful series of novels which were admired by Gladstone and Oscar Wilde, among others. She is remember as much for the imagination and eccentricity of her inventions as for being the first truly popular romantic novelist. Though her work had gone out of fashion long before she died, its spirit lives on. For many years, her home was Killiecrankie Cottage.

KILLIECRANKIE COTTAGE. 5508 J.V.

BEN-Y-GLOE AND BLAIR ATHOLL FROM TULLOCH HILL   968

ATHOLL is one of the most ancient and important divisions of old Scotland. It is one of the original seven earldoms into which the country was divided, such as Fife and Lothian, though a continuing policy of clearance in the last century has meant it lacks their population.

The area includes a large part of the Central Highland massif, many Munros and the Forest of Atholl which is one of the largest deer forests in Scotland, whose herds can often be seen on the verges of the A9.

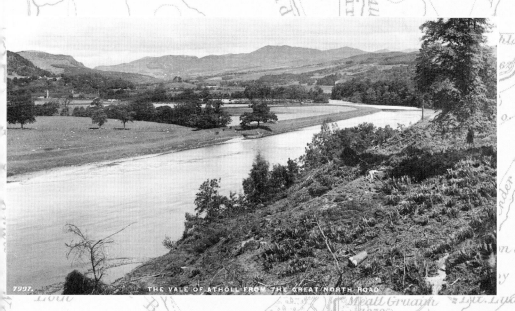

THE VALE OF ATHOLL FROM THE GREAT NORTH ROAD

ATHOLL HIGHLANDERS PIPE BAND, BLAIR CASTLE. STAR PHOTOS COPYRIGHT.

The Murrays held the highest rank in the Scottish peerage and briefly enjoyed full regal powers, though not on the British mainland. In 1736 they inherited the sovereignty of the Isle of Man, giving them the right to summon parliament and issue coinage. The third Duke of Atholl sold his sovereignty to the Crown in 1765, though the Manx three-legged heraldic device still appears on the Atholl coat of arms.

The **ATHOLL HIGHLANDERS** are the last surviving symbol of regal power. They are the only legally permitted weapon bearing private army in the country. Raised in their present form in 1839, their colours were presented to Queen Victoria when she visited Blair Castle in 1845.

BLAIR CASTLE is the seat of the Clan Murray and though greatly altered throughout the centuries, it still retains the thirteenth century Comyn's Tower. It is the last castle in Britain to have been sieged, when Lord George Murray, Charles Edward Stewart's Lieutenant-General, beseiged a government force in his former home for seventeen days in 1746.

BLAIR CASTLE AND BEINN MHEANAIDH,
FROM TULLICH HILL, BLAIR ATHOLL.

The west front of Blair Castle

Properly known as **BLAIR-IN-ATHOLL**, the village starts at the castle gates, where the River Tilt joins the Garry.

GLEN TILT follows the River Tilt from Blair Atholl to its source in Loch Tilt. A drovers' path follows the glen into Braemar and the Cairngorms.

G UP GLEN TILT, BLAIR ATHOLL.

47 IN GLEN TILT, BLAIR ATHOLL.—JUDGES

In 1787, ROBERT BURNS stayed with the Duke and Duchess of Atholl. As a thank-you note he penned the *Humble Petition of Bruar Water to the Noble Duke of Atholl* where he has the river suggest trees would improve its surroundings. Within 10 years the Duke had planted the hillside with 120,000 larch and Scots pine.

MIDDLE FALLS OF BRUAR

Motorists used to be warned their was neither petrol nor anything else for 20 miles beyond **CALVINE**. And an unstated warned was found in the local garage, which used to be piled with cars wrecked on the Drumochter Pass.

THE GREAT NORTH

CALVINE VILLAGE, NEAR STRUAN

STRUAN, BEN-Y-VRACKIE IN THE DISTANCE. 7994.

D 2012

THE GREAT NORTH ROAD NEAR DALNASPIDAL

207960 J.V.

General Wade completed the road between Perth and Inverness in 1729. The commemorative Wade Stone is still on the southbound side of the A9 between **DALNACARDOCH** and **DALNASPIDAL**.

At 1,500 feet above sea level, the **DRUMOCHTER PASS** is the highest point of the A9. Even on the newly engineered road, heavy vehicles struggle to the top.

Two hills face each other across the summit, where Perthshire ends. The larger Sow of Atholl outstares the Boar of Badenoch.

The Great North Road approaching the Pass of Drumocher

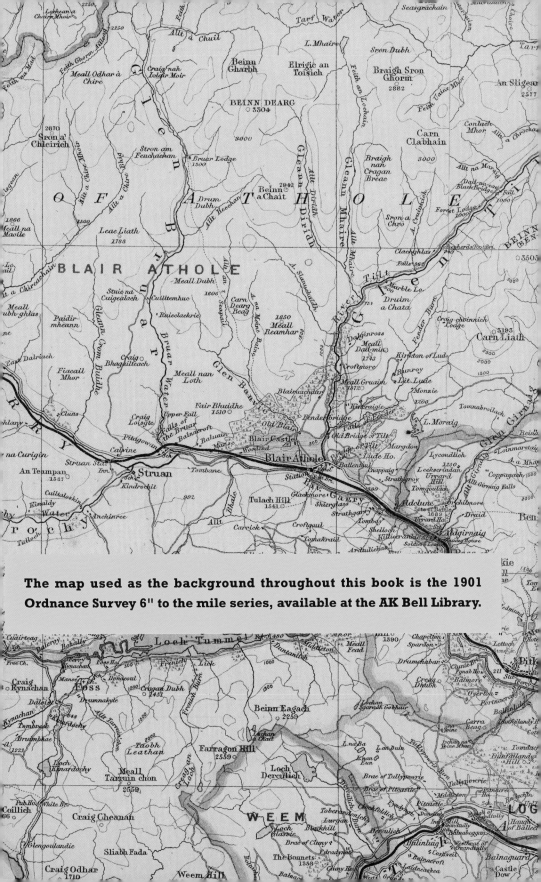

The map used as the background throughout this book is the 1901 Ordnance Survey 6" to the mile series, available at the AK Bell Library.

ONE MILE
TO
CALVINE

Really, a charming quiet retreat.

PERTH &
KINROSS
COUNCIL

ISBN 0 905452 32 1